.32

J 917.2   AUG 22 2019

Winchester Public Library
Winchester, MA 01890
781-721-7171
www.winpublib.org

D1511425

MEXICO

by Jeri Cipriano

LOOK!
BOOKS™

Red Chair Press   Egremont, Massachusetts

Look! Books are produced and published by Red Chair Press:

Red Chair Press LLC   PO Box 333   South Egremont, MA 01258-0333

www.redchairpress.com

Publisher's Cataloging-In-Publication Data

Names: Cipriano, Jeri S.

Title: Mexico / by Jeri Cipriano.

Description: Egremont, Massachusetts : Red Chair Press, [2019] | Series: Look! books : Hello neighbor | Interest age level: 004-008. | Includes index, Now You Know fact boxes, a glossary and resources for further reading. | Summary: "Like any neighbor, Mexico and the United States are alike in many ways and different in many ways. The book compares food, money, national symbols and more. Readers will learn how children in Mexico celebrate holidays that are much like those in the U.S."--Provided by publisher.

Identifiers: ISBN 9781634403269 (library hardcover) | ISBN 9781634403689 (paperback) | ISBN 9781634403313 (ebook)

Subjects: LCSH: Mexico--Social life and customs--Juvenile literature. | Mexico--Description and travel--Juvenile literature. | United States--Social life and customs--Juvenile literature. | United States--Description and travel--Juvenile literature. | CYAC: Mexico--Social life and customs. | Mexico--Description and travel. | United States--Social life and customs. | United States--Description and travel.

Classification: LCC F1208.5 .C56 2019 (print) | LCC F1208.5 (ebook) | DDC 972 [E]--dc23

LCCN: 2017963400

Copyright © 2019 Red Chair Press LLC
RED CHAIR PRESS, the RED CHAIR and associated logos are registered trademarks of Red Chair Press LLC.

All rights reserved. No part of this book may be reproduced, stored in an information or retrieval system, or transmitted in any form by any means, electronic, mechanical including photocopying, recording, or otherwise without the prior written permission from the Publisher. For permissions, contact info@redchairpress.com

Photo credits: iStock except for the following; P. 10, 11, 15, 22: Dreamstime; p.10: Cal Sport Media/Alamy; p. 17: Michele Falzone/Alamy; p. 23: Xinhua/Alamy

Printed in the United States of America

0918 1P CGS19

Table of Contents

All About Mexico

Hola! (OH-la) *Hola* is Spanish for "hello." Many people in Mexico speak Spanish. Mexico is a neighbor to the United States.

Good to Know

There are 64 **national languages** in Mexico. Spanish is the most widely used.

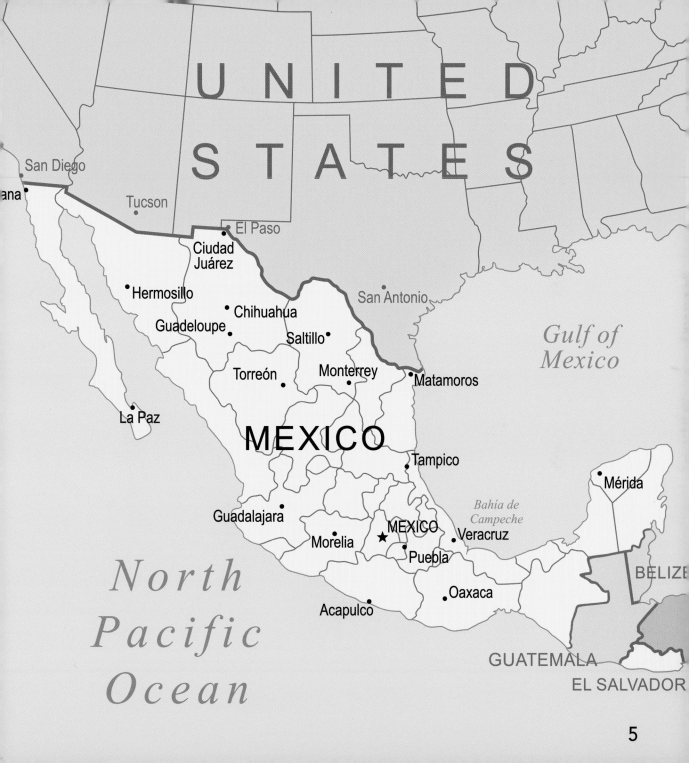

UNITED STATES

San Diego

Tucson

ana

El Paso

Ciudad
Juárez

Hermosillo

San Antonio

Chihuahua

Guadeloupe

*Gulf of
Mexico*

Saltillo

Torreón

Monterrey

Matamoros

La Paz

MEXICO

Tampico

Mérida

Guadalajara

*Bahía de
Campeche*

MEXICO

Morelia

★

Veracruz

Puebla

North

Oaxaca

BELIZE

Acapulco

GUATEMALA

Pacific

EL SALVADOR

Ocean

5

The flag of Mexico is green, white, and red. It shows an eagle with a snake in its mouth. The eagle sits on a cactus.

Good to Know

The U.S. flag has stars and stripes. Do you know what they stand for?

Green is for **Hope**, a peaceful future.
White stands for **Unity**, all for one nation.
Red is for the **Blood** of heroes.

Mexico's **capital** is
Mexico City.

The golden eagle is
Mexico's national bird.

Mexican coins and bills
are called *pesos*. [PAY-sohz]

The most popular sport is **soccer**. In Mexico, it is called *fútbol*.

The sport of rodeo is also popular. Cowboys ride cattle and do rope tricks.

Good to Know

Some U.S. soccer clubs have star players from Mexico. Erick Torres plays for the Houston Dynamo.

The Land and People

Mexico is home to the Mayan people. Mayans have lived in Mexico for thousands of years. Buildings built long ago by Mayans still stand.

Good to Know

The Maya people developed a calendar that is one of the most accurate ever!

This pyramid has 365 steps, one for each day of the year.

Mexico has high mountains.
Mexico also has deep canyons.
The highest peak in
Mexico is Pico de
Orizaba. It is the
tallest **volcano** in
North America.

The Urique (ooh–REE-kay) Canyons are deeper than the Grand Canyon.

Celebrations

Mexico became free from Spain in 1821. <u>Independence Day</u> is on September 16. People march in parades. They dance to folk music.

Good to Know

July 4th is Independence Day in the U.S. This is when the U.S. became free from Britain. How do you **celebrate**?

Children dress in costume for a parade.

The <u>Day of the Dead</u> is on November 1 and 2. Mexicans think of those who died. It is not a sad time. It is a happy time. It is a time to celebrate life. People dress as skeletons. They eat candy skulls.

Good to Know

Can you name a holiday in the U.S. when people might dress like ghosts or skeletons?

April 30 is <u>Children's Day</u>. In Mexico it is called Día del Niño. Children celebrate in school. Stores put toys on sale. Some people think every day should be Children's Day!

Words to Keep

capital: the city that is home to the government

celebrate: come together for a happy reason

national: having to do with a country or nation

soccer: a game in which players use their feet to move the ball (no hands allowed!)

volcano: a mountain that releases lava and hot gases

Learn More at the Library

Books (Check out these books to learn more.)

Moon, Walt K. *Let's Explore Mexico.* (Bumba Books). Lerner, 2017.

Perkins, Chloe. *Living in… Mexico.* Simon Spotlight, 2016.

Robinson, Joanna J. *Mexico.* Child's World, 2015.

Web Sites (Ask an adult to show you this web site.)

Kids' World Travel Guide
www.kids-world-travel-guide.com/mexico-facts.html

National Museum of the American Indian
https://maya.nmai.si.edu/the-maya/maya-people

Index

About the Author

Jeri Cipriano has written and edited many books for young readers. She likes making new friends from different places. Jeri lives and writes in New York state.